THE LI
BOOK
FUNNY
FOREIGN
PHRASES

THE LITTLE BOOK OF FUNNY FOREIGN PHRASES

Copyright © Octopus Publishing Group Limited, 2025

Text by Holly Brook-Piper

An Hachette UK Company
www.hachette.co.uk

Summersdale Publishers
Part of Octopus Publishing Group Limited
Carmelite House
50 Victoria Embankment
LONDON
EC4Y 0DZ
UK

www.summersdale.com

The authorized representative in the EEA is Hachette Ireland, 8 Castlecourt Centre, Dublin 15, D15 XTP3, Ireland (email: info@hbgi.ie)

Printed and bound in China

ISBN: 978-1-83799-549-3

This FSC® label means that materials used for the product have been responsibly sourced

MIX
Paper | Supporting responsible forestry
FSC® C016973

Substantial discounts on bulk quantities of Summersdale books are available to corporations, professional associations and other organizations. For details contact general enquiries: telephone: +44 (0) 1243 771107 or email: enquiries@summersdale.com.

THE LITTLE BOOK OF

FUNNY FOREIGN PHRASES

Sid Finch

summersdale

Note

These translations are correct
to the best of our knowledge.

INTRODUCTION

Sometimes there are occasions when stating the obvious just isn't adequate – the only thing that will suffice is a weird and wonderful phrase to fully embody the situation! Why simply say something is delicious when instead you can describe the food *as if an angel is peeing on your tongue*? Is it early in the morning, or is it *before the pig farts*? Within this book, discover how varied and interesting languages across the globe can be and chuckle at this hilarious (and creative!) collection of quirky phrases and sayings that will help you perfectly express your feelings when you need to go the extra mile!

SWEDISH

Att glida in på en räkmacka

TRANSLATION

To slide in on a shrimp sandwich

MEANING

When someone hasn't had to work to get to where they are or has had everything easy in life

GERMAN

Tomaten auf den Augen haben

TRANSLATION

You have tomatoes on your eyes

MEANING

When you're not seeing or aren't aware of what is happening around you

CROATIAN

Muda labudova

TRANSLATION

Balls of a swan

MEANING

Referring to something
that's impossible

七窍生烟
(qī qiào shēng yān)

To emit smoke from
seven orifices

To be really angry

FRENCH

Avoir d'autres chats à fouetter

TRANSLATION

To have other cats to whip

MEANING

To have other things to do

PORTUGUESE

Barata tonta

TRANSLATION

Dizzy cockroach

MEANING

To be clumsy or disoriented

ITALIAN

Avere gli occhi foderati di prosciutto

TRANSLATION

Having eyes lined with ham

MEANING

Not being able to see something obvious or that's right in front of you

DUTCH

Alsof er een engeltje over je tong piest

TRANSLATION

As if an angel is peeing
on your tongue

MEANING

This food is delicious

BRAZILIAN

Estou cagando e andando

TRANSLATION

I am sh*tting and walking

MEANING

I don't care

GERMAN

Alles hat ein Ende, nur die Wurst hat zwei

TRANSLATION

Everything has an end, only the sausage has two

MEANING

Everything comes to an end

INDONESIAN

Tong kosong nyaring bunyinya

TRANSLATION

An empty barrel makes
the loudest sound

MEANING

Those that know little
tend to talk a lot

FINNISH

Ennen sian pieremää

TRANSLATION

Before the pig farts

MEANING

Early in the morning

PORTUGUESE

É de cair o cu da bunda

TRANSLATION

The asshole falls from the ass

MEANING

When something unbelievable happens

GERMAN

Ich glaub, mein Schwein pfeift!

TRANSLATION

I think my pig is whistling!

MEANING

To exclaim disbelief or indignation, usually at something absurd or unexpected

CHINESE

脱裤子放屁

(tuō kù zi fàng pì)

TRANSLATION

To take off your
trousers and fart

MEANING

To do something
unnecessary

SPANISH

*Gato con guantes
no caza ratones*

TRANSLATION

A cat with gloves does
not catch mice

MEANING

You need the right equipment
to carry out a task

DUTCH

Of je worst lust?

TRANSLATION

Do you like sausage?

MEANING

When someone hasn't been listening and asks for the information to be repeated

ITALIAN

Trattare a pesci in faccia

TRANSLATION

To treat you with fish in your face

MEANING

To disrespect or treat
someone badly

CHINESE

对牛弹琴

(duì niú tán qín)

TRANSLATION

Playing an instrument to a cow

MEANING

When something is being presented to an audience who aren't intelligent enough to comprehend or appreciate it

ARABIC

الشوربة ينفخ في الزبادي
اللي يتلسع من

(allly yatalasae min alshuwrbat yanfukh fi alzibadi)

TRANSLATION

Whoever gets burned by
soup blows on yoghurt

MEANING

If you've been hurt, you're more
cautious the second time

GERMAN

Aus einer Mücke einen Elefanten machen

TRANSLATION

To make an elephant
out of a mosquito

MEANING

To make a big deal out of
a minor inconvenience

FRENCH

Les carottes sont cuites

TRANSLATION

The carrots are cooked

MEANING

The situation is decided
and can't be changed

SWEDISH

Finns det hjärterum så finns det stjärterum

TRANSLATION

If there is room in the heart, there is room for the bottom

MEANING

If you're a good friend, room will be made for you to join in

POLISH

Słoń nastąpił ci na ucho?

TRANSLATION

Did an elephant stomp on your ear?

MEANING

You have no ear for music

กำขี้ดีกว่ากำตด
(kả k̄hî dī kẁā kả td)

TRANSLATION

Grabbing poo is better
than clenching a fart

MEANING

Having something in your hands
is better than having nothing

LATVIAN

Pūst pīlītes

TRANSLATION

To blow little ducks

MEANING

To talk nonsense or to lie

GERMAN

Die beleidigte Leberwurst spielen

TRANSLATION

To play the insulted liver sausage

MEANING

Referring to someone who
is sulking unnecessarily

FRENCH

Avoir le cul entre deux chaises

TRANSLATION

To have your ass
between two chairs

MEANING

Being indecisive and not choosing
between two different options

SPANISH

No tener pelos en la lengua

TRANSLATION

To not have hairs
on your tongue

MEANING

To tell it like it is

ไก่เห็นตีนงู งูเห็นนมไก่

(kị̀ hěn tīn ngū ngū hěn nm kị̀)

TRANSLATION

The hen sees the snake's feet and the snake sees the hen's chest

MEANING

Two people know each other's secrets

ARABIC

القرد في عين أمه غزال

(alqird fi eayn
'umuh ghazal)

TRANSLATION

The monkey is a gazelle in
the eyes of its mother

MEANING

Beauty is in the eye
of the beholder

FRENCH

Donner sa langue au chat

TRANSLATION

To give your tongue to a cat

MEANING

To give up or stop guessing

Auf einem Bein kann man nicht stehen

There is no standing on one leg

One drink is not enough –
you need to have two

POLISH

Z choinki się urwałeś?

TRANSLATION

Did you fall from the
Christmas tree?

MEANING

When someone doesn't know
what they're talking about

JAPANESE

猫をかぶる
(neko o kaburu)

TRANSLATION

To wear a cat on your head

MEANING

Referring to someone pretending
to be something they're not or
hiding their true intentions

PORTUGUESE

Tirar o cavalinho da chuva

TRANSLATION

Take your little horse
out of the rain

MEANING

To give up on something because
it's never going to happen

CROATIAN

Doće maca na vratanca

TRANSLATION

The cat will come to the door

MEANING

The consequences of your actions will come back to haunt you

FRENCH

Avoir la moutarde qui monte au nez

TRANSLATION

To have mustard going
up your nose

MEANING

To lose your temper

GERMAN

Leben wie die Made im Speck

TRANSLATION

Living like the maggot in bacon

MEANING

To live a life of luxury

RUSSIAN

Дать зуб
(dat' zub)

TRANSLATION

To give a tooth

MEANING

To not break a promise

KOREAN

똥 묻은 개가 겨 묻은
개 나무란다
*(ttong mud-eun gaega gyeo
mud-eun gae namulanda)*

TRANSLATION

A dog smeared with poo
scolds a dog covered in bran

MEANING

You shouldn't criticize
someone for their faults
without considering your own

GREENLANDIC

Tulukkat qaqortippata

TRANSLATION

When the ravens turn white

MEANING

It's never going to happen

FRENCH

Péter plus haut que son cul

TRANSLATION

To fart higher than your ass

MEANING

To be arrogant or to think you're above everyone else

DUTCH

Nu komt de aap uit de mouw

TRANSLATION

Now the monkey comes
out of the sleeve

MEANING

When the truth is revealed, or
something suddenly becomes clear

SPANISH

Mi media naranja

TRANSLATION

My half orange

MEANING

My soulmate

PORTUGUESE

Ter macaquinhos na cabeça

TRANSLATION

To have little monkeys inside your head

MEANING

To have a strange or "out there" idea

RUSSIAN

*Дружба дружбой,
а табачок, врозь*
*(druzhba druzhboy,
a tabachok-vroz)*

TRANSLATION

Friendship is friendship, but
let's keep our tobacco apart

MEANING

There's a limit to friendship

GERMAN

Die Katze im Sack kaufen

TRANSLATION

To buy a pig in a poke

MEANING

To buy something without knowing its value or inspecting it first, or to get involved in something unknown

IRISH

Is fánach an áit a bhfaighfeá gliomach

TRANSLATION

What an odd place
to find a lobster

MEANING

It's a small world

GERMAN

*Ich verstehe
nur Bahnhof*

TRANSLATION

I only understand train station

MEANING

I have no idea what
you're on about!

FRENCH

Sauter du coq à l'âne

TRANSLATION

To jump from the rooster
to the donkey

MEANING

To suddenly change the
subject or to jump between
topics in a conversation

RUSSIAN

Хоть кол на голове теши

(khot' kol na golove teshi)

TRANSLATION

You can sharpen a stake on top of his head with an axe

MEANING

Referring to an incredibly stubborn or obtuse person

Da che pulpito viene la predica

Look at the pulpit that sermon's coming from

You're not really in a position to make that comment

PORTUGUESE

Se me fue el avión

TRANSLATION

The plane got away from me

MEANING

I forgot or lost my
train of thought

LATVIAN

Ej bekot

TRANSLATION

Go pick mushrooms

MEANING

Leave me alone

BRAZILIAN

Descascar o abacaxi

TRANSLATION

To peel a pineapple

MEANING

To solve a problem

CHILEAN

Saltó lejos el maní

TRANSLATION

Look how far the peanut jumped

MEANING

Mind your own business

ขี่ช้างจับตั๊กแตน

*(kèe cháang jàp
dták-gà-dtaen)*

TRANSLATION

Ride an elephant to
catch a grasshopper

MEANING

To put in a lot of unnecessary
effort and get little in return

DUTCH

Helaas pindakaas

TRANSLATION

Unfortunately, peanut butter

MEANING

That's too bad

PORTUGUESE

Pagar o pato

TRANSLATION

Pay the duck

MEANING

To take the blame for
something you didn't do

AFRIKAANS

Jy krap met ń kort stokkie aan ń Leeu se balle

TRANSLATION

To scratch a lion's balls
with a short stick

MEANING

To push your luck or be arrogant

POLISH

Bułka z masłem

TRANSLATION

It's a roll with butter

MEANING

It's really easy

ARABIC

العين ماتعلاش عالحاجب

*(il-ein mate'laash
'aal haajib)*

TRANSLATION

The eye doesn't go
higher than the brow

MEANING

No one can go higher
than their status in life

SWEDISH

*Det är ingen
ko på isen*

TRANSLATION

There's no cow on the ice

MEANING

There's no need to worry,
everything is under control

CHILEAN

Chuparse los bigotes

TRANSLATION

Lick your moustache

MEANING

This food is really tasty

WELSH

Fel hwch ar y rhew

TRANSLATION

Like a pig on the ice

MEANING

To look silly

FRENCH

Chier une pendule

TRANSLATION

To sh*t a clock

MEANING

To make a big deal out of
something insignificant

SPANISH

*¡Me cago en
la leche!*

TRANSLATION

I crap in the milk!

MEANING

Damn it!

PORTUGUESE

Dá Deus nozes a quem não tem dentes

TRANSLATION

God gives nuts to those
who don't have teeth

MEANING

Referring to someone who
doesn't make use of an
opportunity they're given

SWEDISH

Skägget i brevlådan

TRANSLATION

Caught with your beard
in the letterbox

MEANING

To be caught in the act

SPANISH

Trabajas menos que el sastre de Tarzán

TRANSLATION

You work less than Tarzan's tailor

MEANING

You're incredibly lazy

GERMAN

Korinthenkacker

TRANSLATION

Currant pooper

MEANING

Referring to someone who is obsessed with trivial details or is pedantic

Skita i det
blå skåpet

TRANSLATION

To sh*t in the blue cupboard

MEANING

To cross the line or to
make a fool of yourself

Más aburrido que bailar con la hermana

TRANSLATION

More boring than dancing
with your sister

MEANING

It's incredibly dull

GERMAN

Kummerspeck

TRANSLATION

Grief bacon

MEANING

Referring to excess weight
put on by emotional eating

FRENCH

Ça ne casse pas trois pattes à un canard

TRANSLATION

It does not break three
legs of a duck

MEANING

It's nothing to write home about,
or it's nothing out of the ordinary

FINNISH

Nakit silmillä

TRANSLATION

To have small sausages
on your eyes

MEANING

To be very drunk

IRISH

Giorraíonn beirt bóthar

TRANSLATION

Two people shorten a road

MEANING

With someone by your side, the journey becomes easier

GERMAN

Hüftgold

TRANSLATION

Hip gold

MEANING

Love handles or weight
carried on the hips

FRENCH

Le cigare au bord des lèvres

TRANSLATION

The cigar is at the tip of the lips

MEANING

I need to poo

ITALIAN

Cavoli riscaldati

TRANSLATION

Reheated cabbage

MEANING

Attempting to revive a failed
relationship often leads
to disappointment

GERMAN

Das ist mir Wurst

TRANSLATION

This is sausage to me

MEANING

I'm indifferent about what's being said (or a certain situation or outcome)

SERBIAN

Nosom para oblake

TRANSLATION

Tearing clouds with their nose

MEANING

Referring to someone who
thinks highly of themselves
or is conceited

ARMENIAN

Գլուխս մի՛ արդուկեր
(klookys mee artooger)

TRANSLATION

Stop ironing my head

MEANING

Stop annoying me

GERMAN

Das Leben ist kein Ponyhof

TRANSLATION

Life is not a pony farm

MEANING

Life can be hard and sometimes things don't go the way you want them to

SPANISH

Tirar la casa por la ventana

TRANSLATION

Throw the house out
of the window

MEANING

To go all out

ITALIAN

Ci sono quattro gatti

TRANSLATION

There are four cats

MEANING

There aren't many people here

GERMAN

*Zwei Dumme,
ein Gedanke*

TRANSLATION

Two stupid people, one thought

MEANING

Fools seldom differ

THE LITTLE BOOK OF FOREIGN SWEAR WORDS

ISBN: 978-1-78783-769-0

Ever been lost for words abroad?

When you want to get your point across
abroad there's only one way to do it:
by swearing your ar*e off! Impress the
world with a stream of multi-lingual
profanity from this nifty pocket book.